FRESH OUT OF THE SKY

George Szirtes was born in Budapest in 1948, and came to England with his family after the 1956 Hungarian Uprising. He was educated in England, training as a painter, and has always written in English. In recent years he has worked as a translator of Hungarian literature.

His first collection, *The Slant Door*, was awarded the Geoffrey Faber Prize, and since then he has won the T.S. Eliot Prize and a Cholmondeley Award and been shortlisted for Whitbread and Forward Poetry Prizes. He was elected a Fellow of the Royal Society of Literature in 1982.

After his first return to Hungary in 1984 he translated poetry, fiction and plays from the Hungarian and for his work in this field he has won the European Poetry Translation Prize, the Dery Prize and been shortlisted for the Weidenfeld and Aristeion Prizes as well as receiving the Golden Star medal of the Hungarian republic. His translation of László Krasznahorkai's *Satantango* won the Best Translated Book Award in 2013, and was a Man Booker International winner in 2015, as translator of László Krasznahorkai.

With George Gömöri he co-edited Bloodaxe's *The Colonnade of Teeth: Modern Hungarian Poetry* (1996), and his Bloodaxe edition of Ágnes Nemes Nagy's poetry, *The Night of Akhenaton: Selected Poems* (2004), was a Poetry Book Society Recommended Translation.

His Bloodaxe poetry titles include: *The Budapest File* (2000); *An English Apocalypse* (2001); *Reel* (2004), winner of the T.S. Eliot Prize; *New & Collected Poems* (2008); *The Burning of the Books and other poems* (2009); *Bad Machine* (2013); *Mapping the Delta* (2016) and *Fresh Out of the Sky* (2021). *The Burning of the Books* and *Bad Machine* were both shortlisted for the T.S. Eliot Prize. *Bad Machine* and *Mapping the Delta* were both Poetry Book Society Choices. Bloodaxe has also published his Newcastle/Bloodaxe Poetry Lectures, *Fortinbras at the Fishhouses: Responsibility, the Iron Curtain and the sense of history as knowledge* (2010), and John Sears' critical study, *Reading George Szirtes* (2008). His memoir of his mother, *The Photographer at Sixteen* (MacLehose Press, 2019), won the James Tait Black Prize for Biography.

Szirtes lives in Norfolk and is a freelance writer, having retired from teaching at the University of East Anglia.

GEORGE SZIRTES

Fresh Out of the Sky

BLOODAXE BOOKS

ISBN: 978 1 78037 584 7

First published 2021 by
Bloodaxe Books Ltd,
Eastburn,
South Park,
Hexham,
Northumberland NE46 1BS

Supported using public funding by
ARTS COUNCIL
ENGLAND

www.bloodaxebooks.com
For further information about Bloodaxe titles
please visit our website and join our mailing list
or write to the above address for a catalogue.

Cover design: Neil Astley & Pamela Robertson-Pearce.

Printed in Great Britain by Bell & Bain Limited, Glasgow, Scotland, on
acid-free paper sourced from mills with FSC chain of custody certification.

For those who leave

ACKNOWLEDGEMENTS

Acknowledgements are due to the editors of the following magazines and anthologies where some of the poems have appeared: *Arrival at Elsewhere* (Against the Grain, 2020), *The Blue Nib, Cordite* (Australia), *The Fenland Reed, Magma, Manhattan Review* (USA), *Meridian* (USA), *The Modernist Bestiary* (UCL Press, 2020), *The New Statesman, Poetry* (USA), *Poetry and Covid-19* (Shearsman, 2020), *The Scores, Singing in the Dark* (Penguin Vintage, 2020), *Verse Daily* and *Write Where We Are Now* (ed. Carol Ann Duffy, Manchester Writing School, 2020).

CONTENTS

FRESH OUT OF THE SKY

1 *Waking to the Sea*

15 Fresh out of the sky
16 Boarding house
17 A cigarette
18 Waking to the sea
19 Meet the parents

2 *London Calling*

20 Fairy tale
21 A wasp in the ear
22 Dream house
23 Neighbour
24 Christmas scene

3 *Tom Brown's Schooldays*

25 Russian incident
26 Diesel or steam
27 Early Christian
28 Table manners
29 Matinee

4 *An Age of Heroes*

30 Tame sparrow
31 The romantic at nine
32 Romance of Munich
33 Dan Dare, Pilot of the Future
34 The cartoon version

5 *The Weather Forecast*

35 Peasouper
36 English rain
37 Wind of change
38 Cricket on Brighton Beach
39 The big freeze

INSIDE THE YELLOW ROOM

43   The Yellow Room
52   Migrant
56   Variations on Leopold Staff
57   One nation

GOING VIRAL

61   *Uncle Zoltán's plague times*
61   *Virus*

Arrival
62   Cruiser
62   Crush
63   Night train
63   Fragment
64   Night patrol

Telling stories
65   Obverse
65   The dream animals return
66   Legend
66   Tradition
67   Growing wild

Creatures
68   Dishes and spoons
68   The pigeons
69   The parrots
69   The penguins
70   The rats

Night Watch
71   River
71   Dusk talk
72   Watchmaker

72   Like clockwork

73   The gates

In the streets of a small town

74   Parchment

74   Ennui

75   The streets of a small town

75   Stopping train

76   Love poem in plague time

Adding up

77   Counting

77   Minutes

78   Trainspotting

78   Figures

79   Where there is sorrow

In wartime

80   Speech bubble

80   Wartime

81   The enemy

81   Disasters of war

82   Ministry

In emergency

83   Emergency guide

83   Dry hands

84   The future

84   Fictions

85   Science fiction

Uncertain terms

86   The angel of uncertainty

86   Addressing the nation

87   Comic turn

87   Ozymandias

88   Anger

After we died

89   Lush
89   Bargain
90   Mouth
90   Blossom
91   After we died

The consolations

92   Gift wrapped
92   Sylph
93   Diaphanous
93   Glory
94   Unscripted

FIVE INTERLUDES

97   In praise of breathing
100   Hen Harrier
102   Morning song
103   Bear
105   Dotage

NINE DREAM SONGS

109   Dream of the future tense
110   Dream of leaving
111   Dream of delay
112   Dream of townscape
114   Dream of screaming
115   Dream of dystopia
116   Dream of television
117   Dream of Moldova
118   Dream of the Danube

BESTIARY

121 Orpheus

122 Ass

123 Lion

124 Stag Beetle

125 Fire Lion

126 Ram skull

127 Toad

128 Chauve souris

129 Owl as anagram

130 Ant

131 Ram

132 Emerging life form

133 Chained beast

134 Tortoise

FRESH OUT OF THE SKY

1 *Waking to the Sea*

Fresh out of the sky

Where to begin? Emerging from the plane
into the winter evening in an age
of winters, of strong winds and a sharp rain

that sweeps along the tarmac, a blank page
to walk across with more pages to come
through distances impossible to gauge,

formalities and waiting and a numb
half expectation as we stand in line
or squat on benches with a constant hum

of meaning that our ears cannot define.
We're fresh out of the sky and here is land,
our very presence part-chance, part-design.

I can't quite conjure it. I seem to stand
at an angle to my life. I cannot see
myself or tell how much of this was planned.

We're citizens of nowhere? Yes, maybe,
but of the world? We're not even quite *here*.
Outside, the rain. The brief formality

of entering the weather. Then a clear
nothing that is both static and moves on
beyond the moment. So we disappear

onto the bus that fills and is soon gone.

Boarding house

Dark corridors, crammed bedrooms, stairs that smell
of cigarette smoke and impermanence.
Long days of waiting. Ringing of the bell

that calls us to our dinner. Shillings and pence
that fill the hand. The wallpaper. The pulse
of other people's half-heard arguments.

The landlord's dog. Interminable phone calls
in the lobby. Someone is falling apart,
another's longing to be somewhere else.

You hold on to the street map of your heart
and make yourself at home. You're here at last,
whatever 'here' now means. Now you can start

your childhood again, the world a mythic past
you'll wander into by mistake, the joys
of lost performance with a vanished cast

of now imagined names that other boys
might whisper just to put you in a spin.
It is another language that deploys

the tottering edifice that you live in.
Strangers will come and go, are gone for good.
The bedrooms empty. Here is a new skin

for you to wear in the enchanted wood.

A cigarette

Hard to remember this without the words,
but words are not yet formed and, half controlled,
they sing and squawk and won't be caged like birds.

Words are excessive. Each one seems to fold
into dozens of new patterns. Words are jokes
that have no point. They freeze you in the cold

December wind that blows between vast rocks.
They crowd into your mouth like blocks of ice
that will not melt. Something in them unlocks

you and exposes you. They sting your face
as you walk the prom holding mother's hand.
Eventually they numb and seal your voice.

It's not a universe you understand
but you must master it, its poetry
unutterable, and – as yet – unscanned.

How do you measure this and learn to see
what lies behind it? Here, in this small room,
you will pay dearly for what once was free.

There's nothing to rely on or assume.
Violence is being done. You're torn in half.
In the meeting hall's gathering winter gloom

a boy stubs out a cigarette on a woman's shapely calf.

Waking to the sea

It's too far out, too great an undertaking
even to imagine it plumbed deep
into your chest, its huge heart aching

for what it can't yet have, not while you sleep.
Tuck yourself in. The sea is black as night,
and as invisible, its pitch too steep

to climb or contemplate. Your skin is tight
as the sheets that tie you down, as stiff
as death, but not your death, not yet. Then light

arrives, a thin grey wall of mist, as if
the air itself had risen out of damp,
and hung before you, solid as the cliff

down in the bay. Put on the bedside lamp.
Listen. There it is, that constant roar
that is the bottom line, its thrust and slump

echoing in you, moving under the floor
you stand on. It is the island you can't see
but know is there. You've not been here before,

but now, it seems, it's where you're meant to be.
They'll find you now. There is no place to hide
but in your head with its brief history.

Stand up. It's morning. Time to go outside.

Meet the parents

Where are they now? Where have they ever been?
And where do they belong, if anywhere?
If they are Time then you're the space between

the hours and days that hang in the sea air
and set their lives to quite a different clock.
He's in an office helping to prepare

others much like himself to take up work
in Midlands factories and offices,
assembling parts or shifting warehouse stock,

sharing truncated lives and premises
with those unlike them, learning how to shop
or find a room among bleak terraces.

She's there with you. She's there to wake you up
and to prepare you – and herself – for speech.
She takes you to the high street where you stop

for coffee and cakes. She simply points to each
then says the words. It is her magic act
to conjure what remains beyond your reach.

The streets, the shops, the houses, each exact,
each now defined. But where's her life in this?
Your knowledge is to pile fact on fact:

hers to translate you with her goodnight kiss.

Fairy tale

Hol volt hol nem volt

Somewhere and nowhere, over the deep blue sea
lies the land of the true exemplary tale,
the magic, transformative mystery

to which a hero traditionally must sail.
The rules are different there. You cannot tell
the wicked from the good and if you fail

you are yourself transformed. May it go well,
young voyager. It's time to leave the coast
and venture inland, follow the heady smell

of petrol, paraffin, fog and car exhaust,
down highways to small suburbs with loud schools
with greens and gravy round a greasy roast.

You have your store of words that serve for tools
to work your way into the heart of strange
new darknesses prepared for hapless fools

and oddments such as you. You must arrange
your life to fit and figure a defence.
You won't do as you are so you must change.

You're in the land of plenty and good sense.
You've fallen among the kind. You're wearing shoes.
Now venture further. Seek the future tense

that you must first locate, then freely choose.

A wasp in the ear

A maisonette next to the railway line
in a street no longer there. You scramble down
the steep embankment listening for the train

that even now is steaming into town.
Blackberries, nettles, bindweed, daisy, vetch,
and dandelions with their golden crowns

all tumble down the slope. This is your patch
for now, your small domain, the twilight zone
you see in dreams. Nothing here will etch

itself into your memory. Your memory's gone
or fading fast. Your brother must be there
but, waiting by the track, you're on your own.

One night you feel a buzzing in your ear.
It is a wasp. You put your finger in
and prompt the sting that is the sound of fear

inside your head, a dull incessant din
that stays for weeks. Is this, then, memory?
A set of incidents, a ruptured skin,

a sting? But no. The mind will soon float free
of such, to new domains where nothing's set
in stone or flesh, where things still strive to be.

As Jolson said, *you ain't heard nothing yet.*

Dream house

A barely furnished place, half damp, half shade.
Is that your mind at work, an empty shell
you fill with moments, memories you've made

from glimpses, as you might of a hotel
that's so like dreams it must have been invented?
Invention is what you do, and all too well,

a vague half-space, dubiously scented,
designed to fill an emptiness so faint
it can't even be properly presented.

It's dark all right, and damp, with peeling paint
or is it wallpaper? Too late to know,
too late indeed to register complaint

or blink it back. It's simply where you go
when there is nowhere else, an absent year
in absent lives whose absences will grow

to further absence. But let's mark it here.
We are in Hendon, not far from the station,
in a house already marked to disappear,

in streets now changed beyond all recognition,
at least as you remember them. Assume
whatever self you like, it is all fiction.

Remain just where you are, in that damp room.

Neighbour

Now meet the neighbours. Meet the social grin
under the friendly, non-committal eyes
that look to gauge you, how you might fit in.

You are prepared to see how the land lies,
but it's your house, a whole house, in a row
of others like it, your own Nobel Prize

for being here, a happiness you know
once through the door and standing in the hall,
or out in the back garden where you grow

whatever takes your fancy. It's your call
and no one else's, right up to the fence
that's not quite in the office of a wall.

It's comedy, the laughter of the tense.
You catch the disapproving glance of Jack
next door, who notes your lack of garden sense.

Damn foreigners! he'll mutter. *Can't keep track
of all their comings and goings. It's the war
all over again.* But there's no going back.

And he'll be generous, as once before,
and might be so next year. And he will smile
at you, while at his own back many more

nod you their greeting. *You'll be here a while.*

Christmas scene

Now here is evidence: a photograph
to show real chairs and tables in a room
at one specific time; a world of stuff

that might be traced by any rule of thumb.
Suddenly, it is a British Christmas,
to honour which two families have come

to occupy the same space labelled 'us'.
Two pretty little girls on adult laps
stare out among the understated fuss

of paper decorations like strange maps
now crisped and curled into the simplest shapes
compared to which we are untidy scraps

of this and that. What of the girls? What hopes
for their sweet faces? One dies young,
a tumour gets her. The other one escapes

into a fog and vanishes. How long
before she reappears? You cannot know.
Your questions and your guesses are all wrong.

Elsewhere and everywhere is where we go
with each according to his lot. That's fine.
We do not question it. It is just so.

We are in no man's land, across the line.

3 *Tom Brown's Schooldays*

Russian incident

Boys are kicking a ball in the playground. The ball
lands at your feet as you watch them by the door.
A dull October day. Children huddle

and chase each other. It's what break is for.
You've saved the scene from a discarded clip
of film without deep focus, mostly blur

but with a soundtrack, or a cartoon strip
in which you have a role as just a cry
or vacant talks balloon. But then you skip

the next scene and however hard you try
you cannot splice them, see the pair as one.
You ask to play and are refused. But why?

They think you're Russian, says a boy. Kids run
to and fro. Hungarian, you sniff.
You're eight years old. The action judders on

but now you're playing with them. It's the cliff
off which you've fallen, landing on your feet,
ready to run, the core of your belief

that nothing's changed, that life is one discreet
and undivided package from which you
have just emerged, unruffled, calm, as neat

as truth itself and certified as true.

Diesel or steam

You're standing in the doorway after class
when Jimmy wants to know if you prefer
diesel or steam. You can't simply say pass

and hope to leave. There's no time to defer.
You have to say right now as if you knew
the answer. But what to say? The two things blur

so which to choose? And why did he ask you?
Others are waiting. Nobody explains.
Their eyes are curious. Your answer's due

though you know next to nothing about trains
and engines. So you vaguely plump for steam
and are approved. Now steam runs through your veins

you're of the party. Life becomes a dream
of existential choices. Jimmy's gone.
Out in the playground where your classmates scream

and tussle, odds are million to one
you'll get them right but choices must be made
and loyalties defined. What's done is done.

Diesel is wrong! You have a barricade.
Prepare, Britannia, to face the foe!
Possess your weapons. Do not be afraid

of where the trains divide and where they go.

Early Christian

The consolations of religion are warm milk,
a prayer just before bed, the cosiness
of being tucked up with enticing talk

of God the kind and merciful who'll bless
your sleep and dreams and see you safe at home
when you get back with nothing to confess

and be forgiven for. You learn this from
the teacher who has brought you here, a god
himself, a gift from kingdoms yet to come.

The Isle of Wight. Dear child, beware the rod
and slipper and trust only to the Lord,
and live your life according to his code.

The child had never heard God's mighty word
announced as clear this. It must be true,
a king as kind as this should be adored.

Heaven might open and yet one fall through
into the dark where rod and slipper wait,
with shame and guilt, at simply being you.

So God embraced him in his arms but fate
decreed he should be cast away alone.
Good children speak the truth, are never late,

no rod will ever turn their hearts to stone.

Table manners

This is the way to do it, they advise
with perfectly straight faces, table set
for all the mischief in their childish eyes.

Here's your napkin now. Here's where you sit,
here the theatrical business of the knives
and forks and spoons. Now you may start to eat

the fragile silence into which you'll dive
and breast the currents where you now belong.
A miracle how anyone survives

such comic censure. It's a minor wrong
in minor territory, just a prank
that you yourself will laugh at before long.

Oh manners! All the money in your bank
is there for taking once one gets the key
and knows just when to speak and whom to thank

for silence and that dark fragility.
Arrange your face, prepare your steady hands
for inspection so everyone may see

how clean they are. Collect the various strands
of your being into a neat display
of small perfections, minimal demands

for the great hunger, for some other day.

Matinee

This is the universe with children in it.
They gawp or laugh or scream or flick popcorn
at each other. It is the brilliant broken minute

of their lives, the reason they are born,
an episodic set of propositions
in the dark hall of comedy and scorn.

And here they are now in their set positions,
tenth row back, among the quieter sort,
learning the wild silence of wild visions:

the belly laugh, the tensions, the loud snort
of the brief moment, the best of Saturdays
down at the Gaumont and the keen blood-sport

of childhood which has led them to its maze
of corridors, the underside of school.
Meanwhile the lasso twirls, the music plays,

the cabin's on fire, the manic cartoon fool
pirouettes on a leaf, the singing starts.
It's as if time were on an endless spool

of incidents composed of jagged parts
that will not fit without a show of force.
The morning passes and the crowd departs

under the gaze of a queen on a white horse.

Tame sparrow

We are the soft toys of imagination,
they declare. You'll live with us for ever
as your shadowing, your secret nation.

She longed for such companions to forgive her,
assembled them in cages, fed them from her hands,
and so they sang and flowed like a bright river

delighting the bright house. She gave commands
and they obeyed in their own minimal way
by singing on in choirs and captive bands.

The children had their own time-bound array
of hamsters and white mice and ducks and chicks
to tend to and observe from day to day,

since this was nature they could nurse and fix
so it could nurse them back and fix their dreams
when they were troubled; nature without tricks,

with tiny teeth and beaks, the faintest screams
they'd ever hear. And then the sparrow came
dropping from its nest to perch on thumbs,

fingers and shoulders like a favourite game.
Miraculous! That nature could be free
yet intimate, a creature wild yet tame,

as any one of them might yearn to be.

The romantic at nine

On n'est pas sérieux, quand on a dix-sept ans.

You're not really in love when you are nine,
but you already know what is romance,
you've been there, done it, found there was a line

from dizziness through to the ghostly dance
of something else unnamed. A single look
can send you there, a half-propitious glance

propel you to the pages of a book
you've not yet read where the whole story's told.
Here in the playground that was all it took

to fall in love, for stories to unfold
in languages so foreign even you,
without a language, coming to it cold,

could open wide and vaguely riffle through.
Helen and Wendy, Sarvin, Jenny, Joan,
each stranger than the rest, resplendent, new,

were shining creatures to admire alone.
Was this your country now, the trysting fields
of your own treasure island, having blown

ashore like this? What is the force that shields
you from disaster, since disaster comes
whether you will or no? The stronghold yields.

Desire advances with its muffled drums.

Romance of Munich

The air crash. You remember that. The news.
The grainy photographs. A broken plane.
The snow like blobs of fat, the ground a bruise

turned into sky. There's no need to explain,
it's clear enough what happened. It's the dream
of the disaster you will dream again,

that nothing ever after can redeem.
What, after this, has settled in your mind
except a name, a date, a football team,

a concept that remains still undefined.
Your new romance is with the thing that's lost,
the hour that wipes a slate and is unkind.

And then they rise out of their blood and dust
to reappear as bodies, new for old.
The team remains the team despite the cost.

They fall at the last hurdle but they hold
your foreign hand, so now at last, you're theirs.
They are the reason for that special cold

deep in your bones. But now your love repairs
the crashed machine from which the dead will flow
like air across the field. Here come the heirs

of the young men who haunt you as you grow.

Dan Dare, Pilot of the Future

I saw the Mekon on his flying chair,
his vast green head so crammed with wicked schemes
he seemed all brain, the dark side of the air.

Reptilian Treens would sail through earthling dreams
like products of men's fears, their alien skulls
and fixed expressions like cold-blooded screams

inside the head, tight-lipped through endless battles.
Where was Dan Dare, with his British do or die,
his flying jacket and his unseen medals.

Where was that hook of brow above his eye?
Dear Britain, with your lantern jaw and grit,
your Digby and your glamorous Peabody,

I trusted you, glossy and clear as spit
and polish. This was my Britain of the mind
at nine years old, the crew in my space cockpit,

the sole representatives of mankind
in outer space, a space so much like home
that one might live there, perfectly defined

within a single island aerodrome,
training to be a pilot of the future,
for the extra-terrestrial life that was to come

as swift as vengeance, smooth as second nature.

The cartoon version

The distinction between my cartoon life
and everyday is never an easy one.
It's possible in both to come to grief.

Chaos is the natural order: the fun
side of the reign of terror. Violence
is comical. It's never a real gun

but canes and slippers make a brutal sense.
I'm lost in Bash Street now. An air of menace
hangs by the school gates. My innocence

is cartoon innocence. Out in the yard Dennis
waits for a boy in specs. Back in the house
Dad flexes his muscles while his enemies,

the wild boys, lurk in the garden. Enormous
shadows rise on the wall. A burned out car
smokes on the horizon. A sabre-toothed mouse

grins at a screaming woman. There's nothing bizarre
about any of this. This is life: get used to it.
There's always someone somewhere crying *Aaargh!*

I'm bursting my sides laughing. My football kit
is strewn across the floor. I can hear myself lying
to my parents. I'm Roger the Dodger, fit

to enter the frame, steady, death-defying.

5 *The Weather Forecast*

Peasouper

Sometimes the whole place merges into grey:
lampposts, bollards, shop windows, buses, vanish
into a soup that's neither night nor day

but blankness, like a face without a blemish,
a steamed-up mirror with a picture of nobody,
nothing but fog, nothing from start to finish.

The streets are soaked. Grass verges, slick and muddy,
are slush-filled pulp. You tread through clots
of thickening mist that seems to pulse and eddy

like the sea while tying itself in knots.
Where has everyone gone? Perhaps they've drowned,
or hidden in invisible dark slots

that won't materialise until they're found.
Then one appears, a vague form looming up
then swaying off, an apparition gowned

in fog, discolouration in a half-full cup
of forgotten tea. So spirits one by one
appear then fade at the point where things stop

being things. This then is the fabled London
of the novels, where everyone is lost
in stories that tail off, then carry on

without them, without echo, at no cost.

English rain

This rain, this unremitting stoical drench
that defined everything by fully soaking it
was now home. It was like living in a trench

in a war that never started. Men were smoking it
in offices through rain-blurred windows. They stood
in melancholy doorways, mentally stroking it

as you might a sodden dog. Rain was a hood
you wore in the street and took off once at home.
It was another name for England. It was the good

you lived by for months on end, that would come
on time like buses that once arrived don't go.
This was childhood in winter, the proper medium

for study and squalor, into which you'd grow
like a plant into soil, putting down your roots.
Each shower was eternity, an endless flow

of sustenance and drowning. Pull on your boots,
wear your raincoat. It's winter now for ever.
It is time in one of its worn out old suits,

that glorified gentleman inclined to shiver
and grumble. Meanwhile you watch the children run
through puddles, crossing streets and seeking cover

like something ending that has not begun.

Wind of change

It was Uncle Mac of 'children everywhere'
who first announced it out on the Gold Coast
The wind was going to blow and wouldn't spare

heads of children's entertainment. The Ghost
Of Christmas Past was in the works. No more
Sparky's Magic Piano. Burl Ives was toast.

So Tubby the Tuba had to know the score
like Arthur Askey. Same for Danny Kaye
and Mandy Miller. Whatever happened before

had to stop right now. They'd had their day.
Africa would be free. The Empire would close down
and there'd be no more Michael Holliday.

Instead there would be hurricanes. The Crown
might vanish in an endless summer storm
however the Queen or Prince of Wales might frown.

But Uncle Mac still played the songs, his warm,
comforting voice would always be enough,
and there would still be men in uniform

to keep us marching because no piffling puff
of wind changed that. Albert would meet the Lion
as sure as The Troll met Three Billy Goats Gruff.

Despite the wind that was something to rely on.

Cricket on Brighton Beach

The first time you hear it you are lying bored
on Brighton's pebbled beach. Your parents nearby
have closed their eyes, enjoying their reward

for working through the winter, so you try
the radio, ever so quietly, and come upon
two voices, hardly louder than a sigh,

discussing a game that seems to have begun
several days ago but is happening now,
and seems to have every intention of going on.

England is the raising of an eyebrow,
the tempo of a surgical operation
under anaesthetic. It will end somehow,

some time, like a long official procession,
a suggestion of events grown into coherence
in the process of an endless conversation

under which lies a drama with its own intense
narrative, of which you're not a part.
An injured man is struggling under immense

pressure. The devil steams in to blow him apart.
Or so it seems. Or this is Brighton beach
with nothing on except a form of art

that no one can explain to you or teach.

The big freeze

To be so cold and out of sync, snowed in,
snowed out, trapped as if for ever, white
as if for ever, next to the paraffin

heater that stank of danger every night
was fun at first, then farce, then edge of doom
to watch it pile up, brilliant and bright

fading to brown, sky a permanent gloom.
It was history-as-present where we were
suspended in time, locked inside a room

with England covered, frozen in a blur
of swirling snow, all definition gone.
We were another country, made of fur

and language, with our woolly sweaters on,
layer on layer, in a land of Ice Queen eyes
like frozen darts. Snow was falling by the ton.

If something as soft as this could paralyse
the country what might a fat bomb not do?
It was a land of slippage and surprise.

What wonderful icicles, what splendid new
patterns on glass! We looked on the bright side
of life and knew that somehow we'd get through,

another chapter in the nation's pride.

INSIDE THE YELLOW ROOM

The Yellow Room

Waking in the yellow room

Listen, a creature is stirring in the corner
of the yellow room. Half child – half adult,
it has a name it is called by: *Lah-tsi-ka*.
My father, tenderly addressed by his grave aunt,
moves towards her, as I would, and once did.

But he has already done what I never did,
which is to say he has died. As of course has his aunt
and anyone else addressing him as *Lah-tsi-ka*.
This is the house of the dead you enter as an adult
and leave as the child still squatting in the corner.

*

It is a burning room. A bright yellow room
as seen by Chagall when a child, a desolation
that is, at the same time, rich with its own past;
a room of hush and wail and silent reading;
of newspapers or holy texts or sheets of accounts.

It is a room of which there are few proper accounts
and you are obliged to sit there silently reading
whatever text is presented to you by the past.
I don't think you are thinking of desolation.
To you a room is simply a room, and this is the room.

*

The alarm goes. Get up. You must set off to work.
You're not a child anymore. You must open the door
and step outside into shared streets and shared offices.
You must do your new work, which is what Time
offers you now, right at this moment, this era.

It is simply a moment in an era like any other era.
Life is what it is. You are a creature of your time
and are obliged to perform its perfunctory offices.
I see you moving down the street, up stairs, to a door
with the ghost of a name on. This, for now, is your work.

*

Say no to melodrama, say no
    to self-pity. Say no to cliché, to
            chronicles that bear too heavy a

symbolic load. Say no
    to the role assigned to you. Say no,
            to the assigners who include

    yourself. Say no to the ghetto,

to the ritual you perform on your own memory,
    to the vocabulary you work with. Say no to

        practically everything, to your aunt, to your
mother, your sister, your dead kin, to your
            image in the shaving mirror,

to all rooms including the yellow room.
    Say NO to the yellow room.
    Especially to the yellow room.

Say no say no say no say no say no say no

Start again.

*

Your intimacy strides before you. I can feel it
as soon as you enter the room. It is breath
distilled into need, a gruffness never at home
with itself. It is desire to be loved, to extend
the self into the most intimate of circles.

It is, however, only one of several circles
beyond the room. Such circles should not extend
into private rooms in private flats. They have no home.
They are offices and jails. They are the frozen breath
of ideas you can smell. Here is one. You can feel it

*

touching your neck. It is cold and deadly. You wait
before rising and moving on, calm and determined
to work your passage of innocence. You don't speak
to us about it. You talk a desperately tender language
that emerges out of warm beds and long nights.

Night in the yellow room is just one of many nights:
it is the world's night anywhere. It speaks a language
of endings and awakenings. It is what nature speaks
when contented with what has already been determined.
Everything will be fine, it says, if you just wait.

*

You are waiting to establish your own intimate
landscape. You are waiting to organise your files.
You are waiting for shadows to pass, for the calendar
to fly from the wall and out through the open window.
You are waiting for moments of quiet like this.

This is a quiet moment. There are moments like this
on the tip of the tongue. Now you have opened the window
the sunlight steps in and rearranges the calendar
as a permanent present. These are the yellow room files
on a good day, comfortable, desirable, intimate.

*

I am talking to you as if I could
                              see you
    as a function of my own short-sighted eyes.
I can't quite separate you from the fog
            that surrounds you.

    I am trying to fix you in your own sphere.
I am trying to help you float through
            the ambient air of time. I am
                trying to see how you came to be here

    where I am, as if your eyes looked out through mine.

It's too late for that, you whisper.

The Jewish Quarter

This is the Jewish quarter, latterly the ghetto.
Dozens of shops, small businesses, dead names
between classic bullet-riddled portals
that constitute a history of jokes.
Walk me through there, dad, buy me something.

Introduce me to the tradesmen. Tell me something
I don't know. Guide me through the jokes
you tell at dinner. Pick the bullets from the portals.
Show me the faces. Give them back their names.
Open my eyes. Open the gates of the ghetto.

The Ghetto and the ghetto:
             which one are you leading me through
   and where are the gates?
Where are the ears and eyes and nostrils and fingers
       of the place you would show me?
Will you show me Venice and provide me
             with an introduction to Shylock?
   Is there a shop on the Rialto
       selling pounds of flesh?

             Dear father, these are rhetorical question
but you must know something,
                   even if it is only the map

   or the ghost map

along whose streets you move as I must move in my way
             whether through dreams or in live traffic
the traffic of gesture and hint and silence
   which is my silence

Look the sun is shining through the window of the yellow room
        creating a small slab of brilliant light
that is almost burning the way a bush would,
    though there's nothing in the bush just symbols
        and man does not live by symbols alone

not even in solitary confinement
not even in the ovens such lights configure.

*

The day you set off to the front you could not
take the ghetto with you though at night
you felt its glow emanating from the moon
that was licking the yellow floor of the cabin as if
hungry for dust and fetor and suppuration.

It was perhaps the room itself, the suppuration
mere jaundice and green gall you'll survive if
there's luck on your side, by favour of the moon
that dipped in and out of cloud the whole brief night
in places where you desired to be but were not.

Dust

Your dust is still sitting in its box, not yet scattered
in any place that might have been dear to you,
since we don't know what were the places you dreamt
or hoped for, if indeed there was such a place,
some street or field or room, a house or a bed.

Might it have been the sea, settled on the sea bed
or drifting off on the tide to a generous place
on a distant island, an island I too have dreamt?
Your dust lies heavy on me as if I should carry you
to some coherence though I myself am scattered.

*

Your dust, the camp, the brilliant escape
in the morning fog across fields. How to square
the two? Does dust escape into a freer world
when blown from an open hand? Where does it go?
Where would yours go now if only it could?

Dust does not speak, you say, as if you could.
I have been here some time, now I have to go
out into what may be just another world.
I've left the yellow room, walked out into the square
and watched the dust in the cold air escape.

*

Still the yellow room that is only
                    dust
            in the cold wind, hanging
        for a moment, then gone, like a voice

that has stopped speaking, a room
                in a questionable yellow, a light
that is a lantern constructed out of history,
    a peculiarly yellow history that breathes
                its own yellow dust

dust I cannot quite collect or recollect
    or even conjure by a simple naming. Rain

    falls outside in the square, soft
interminable rain.

                And dust, Right here. Right now.

Ring circuit and stalemate

This isn't going anywhere, you complain,
and you are right. You are stuck in one bad year
and it takes a mighty tug to pull you out.
From here on life will get worse for a while
but you know you will survive, take comfort from that.

But no, there is no comfort to be had from that,
you complain, no comfort, not for a good while.
Stop denying me, I say. Or I'll call you out
as something I've not yet thought of. Next year
maybe I will give you reasons to complain.

*

No point in arguing with the dead, still less so
with yourself. All one makes of that is poetry,
which is no consolation. We are at a standstill
you and I.

          I see you playing cards
in a garden with your friends, a cigarette

in your mouth. You offer me a cigarette.
You show me a handful of foreign cards.
You explain the rules. You sit so very still
it is as though you were composing poetry
in your head but you will not say so.

*

This poem goes round and round and cannot escape.
It has no field. It cannot move beyond the ring
it is bound to. It is circularity of definition.
The yellow room is somewhere at the centre.
People are lighting their lamps there.

How easy might it be to enter there,
to nod to those sitting at the very centre
of the room, certain of their own self-definition
of their secret society, of the familiar ring
of footsteps running and making their escape?

Migrant

1

He woke to find himself next to himself
or it might have been herself, it was hard to be sure.
His face was dissolving or it might have been his eyes
or her eyes or even his skin, and he couldn't remember
his name or anyone else's, such things being dreamlike
right from the beginning, and the bed was snow or an image of snow
and the sound outside was of something completely outside
any outside of which one might once have been sensible.
And there was the mirror, of course, because mirrors
are primary, a mirror no longer him or her or even
quite human but faintly bestial yet helpless
and as much himself as anything had ever been
before it all started, before the body he wore
or inherited was his or hers or, if either's, just a projection
that someone projected.

2

It was a cold morning in winter coming around again
for the tenth or eleventh or sixty-ninth or seventieth time
one without name or identity, simply a presence of which
no one was ever quite sure, a usual, everyday
evanescence of season and presence, not a convincing
model of the potential blossoming into the frozen
air of the future where everything is suspended
in its own hope and desire, in every related condition.
So he rose, or she rose, and they entered the bathroom
together at once like a double-act marooned in its own isolation
and stood at the basin and washed a face
very like someone whose teeth they remembered brushing
though the teeth were gone, mere ghost teeth
in a ghost mouth that was saying something ghostlike
to the dream in front of them, which was a thing

seen in a mirror, and Who have you been? came the question
and there was no answer to be seen or heard.
But this, said the questioner, is your identity,
this your fixed form and the form of the world beyond you.
Go out into it and confront the terrifying question
of its enormous clamouring mouth with its real teeth,
its sickness and grave-clothes, and greet it for me,
just as you are, it is that kind of party, you need not
change anything. And it put on its hat and grinned
and went on its way as any respectable ghost would.

3

So out into the world, to the familiar street
that had never been familiar, past the war memorial
where names yawned at him as they might at a tedious story
that he knew to be tedious since she himself had
told him so often, and there was the cat in the doorway
and two dogs sniffing and the man with the bent back
shuffling towards a corner that was tedious yet strange
as if yanked into daylight just as a shadow suddenly
appears when the sun demands it, and there was
the butcher with his aged hands at the counter
hauling his goods into the light of the window, smiling
at something, at a child with a fistful of ham,
and all was familiar, the child, the ham, the butcher
and the light because it was that kind of party, with sickness
and grave-clothes with the beauty of the street
as footnote or afterthought in which he or she was looking
to enter the world by way of that street and that street only
passing the war memorial and the yawning tedium
of a past that was potentially his for the taking,
so he took it and said, This is my past, this tissue of lies
and inventions, just as the woman with the bicycle
passed him tinkling her bell in a version of madness
that was certainly one of the world's faces, which was
not his face or her face, not even exactly the world's.

4

She rides by and waves, wearing gaudiest colours,
an angel unto herself and the world in her head
that may become the world. She is its avant-garde
avatar and he, or someone else, marvels at her progress
which is historical in the chronicled manner, so she,
so the street, so the world of the mind, where the aged
are rejuvenated and have never grown old. You are ageing,
says the voice in his own head. You too are chronicled
and gaudy and avant-garde, ahead of yourself, speeding
down the street in your angelic livery, in the world
you imagine she imagines. It's a dark place in there
but there are angels and avatars and it's safe in the street
where light constantly shuttles between day and night,
between darkness and safety. Then she is gone
round a corner, into death or the next thing.

5

The next thing is this. It is being addressed by the world
as a next thing. There are too many faces, he thinks
or she thinks, too many presences, alighting as from
a horse in a parallel yet incomprehensible universe.
Why can't a horse be human, he thinks or she thinks,
why must it be alien and extra-planetary? And he notes
horses in a field, ambling into their own graceful
yet lopsided future. Are they too migrants? Could they
have smuggled themselves into the country like shadows
of horses, or traces of horses, equipped with fake documents?
Where is the familiar world in which a horse is a horse
and yet human? Where is the familiar terminology
in which one might address the world as condition?
It is as if there were nothing in the field, she thinks
or he thinks, nothing apart from the wind on the grass
smoothing its back with a tender familiarity
he or she, or she or he remembers from infancy
as a faintly maternal exhalation, a hand through

a window, a smell in a wall, a social something
into which a horse might be dropped as by parachute
and be human and horse-like and hovering above
the field like a shadow becoming itself in the light.

Variations on Leopold Staff

1

I built my house of smoke
And peopled it with fire
Because there must be fire

Within the fire the house
Within the house the smoke
Within the smoke myself

2

He did not trust in bricks and mortar
But the chimney spouted smoke
Down the chimney pigeons purring
Down the chimney raven's croak
Illusion, cried the distant engine
Illusion, he exclaimed, and woke.

3

This too solid flesh might turn to stone
And on that stone a building might be raised
The rest is smoke and mirrors, smoke and gone.

4

These are your foundations.
That is where you begin.
Do not look for meanings.
Do not look for endings.
Begin here. Prepare the fire.

One nation

1

The place hasn't changed. Things are in their place.
Things remain exactly what they were: just things.
Home comforts are what we expect of home.

Sunlight hovers on walls, remaining sunlight
even when spread on pavements. Our keel is more or less even.
Our clothes are comfortable simply because they're our clothes.

Back to front, front to back we go, until we're back
at the front. We try to preserve a united front.
Here is where we are: our place is always here.

2

The softness of the place, the pressing into grass.
The warmth when it arrives in forms of grace.

The soft bricks, the earth that crumbles. Rain
that gentles and does not precipitate ruin.

Temperate climes. Our fingers on the pulse
of dinner and bed, the night fumbling for pills.

3

The poor will get poorer, the rich richer. The wind
of fortune bloweth where it listeth. Justice is blind
and carries a switchblade. We preserve our kind.
Our forces remain alert and disciplined.

We will creep a little closer to the ground.
After today we will face the everyday grind
with less resolution. Things will be defined.
Life will be returned exactly as found.

4

But something will have broken. The broken chair
will litter up the hall. The broken machine will
rust in the shed. Meanwhile jets rise into a sky
where nothing breaks or, when it does, things fall
and break still more. The broken do not fly.
The month begins in pieces on the floor.

GOING VIRAL

Uncle Zoltán's plague times

My Uncle Zoltán
had an eye for disasters.
He'd watch them passing

like a smear of crows
cursing at the failing light.
His gothic nature

sympathised with them,
drunk on the melodrama.
He was facetious.

Sometimes he was right.

Virus

Everything wants life,
said the thing, meaning itself,
we too struggle on.

It was dark by now,
and the stars were fine powder,
almost invisible.

And they did want life
at some expense to others,
but that's nothing new,

it's just fine powder.

Arrival

Cruiser

Somewhere a cruiser
is patrolling the North Sea.
You imagine it

passing the headland,
like your own dream of waking,
just turning over,

not yet quite conscious,
but surfacing from a depth
in the darkness, there,

beyond the shore lights.

Crush

The crush of bodies
and faces. It is as if
they had just emerged

out of an old dream's
familiar narrative.
But who is dreamer,

and who dreamt? They move
as one dream with the tired face
we take home with us

like handfuls of change.

Night train

The night train stops here,
just at that platform. You will
hear it approaching.

Here the journey starts
into that plump-heart darkness
you will not notice.

You will be dreaming
of the carriage and the lights
in the far distance

that sounds like your heart.

Fragment

Something happened there
that was not told in stories
shaped by memory.

Time was part of it.
It no longer ran clear but
was broken music,

fragments of which lay
on the floor, catching the light,
as if it could make

sense of the darkness.

Night patrol

Now the lights are off
and the town is almost dead
the creatures enter

on all fours, or wings,
or sheer force of tongue or mind
to take their due place

in each other's eyes,
in their usual habitat
as dream companions

we half know by name.

Telling stories

Obverse

Somewhere in the sea
there are creatures who worship
a darker full moon,

whose lives are obverse
and mirror wise, who dream of
waking as the dreams

of those on the shore.
Their words are born in the mouth
and live in water

without drowning them.

The dream animals return

Some time, very late,
on a night of the full moon,
their dream animals

returned to feed them
as best they could. So they ate
the animals' gifts,

or imagined them,
because imagination
was edible too,

as was the full moon.

Legend

Once upon a time,
in an age of deities,
they conceived of plagues

that served to reduce
the world they had created.
So goes a story

often repeated.
Meanwhile the planets revolve
in the usual way

with wide open mouths.

Tradition

'Once upon a time...'
they will begin. The old ways
are always the best,

and maybe that is
how we will remember it,
in the old way, yet

never as 'the past'.
A light wind runs down the stream
of the future. Here,

down this street, this lane.

Growing wild

Here's your patch of sky
and here the ground below you.
Here is a window,

walls, ceiling and floor.
Here is a self to play with
when you get bored. Read

the enormous map
that is yours for exploring
with the dense language

that will grow wild now.

Creatures

Dishes and spoons

Everything can change
in a moment, they were warned.
Tall buildings tumbled,

dishes ran away
with spoons, soon there were riots,
carnivals, crackdowns,

and bombs, followed
by a delicious silence.
It was a moment,

and so they moved on.

The pigeons

Here come the pigeons,
comical yet menacing,
strutting in sunlight

across public squares
and small suburban gardens.
How like generals

or dignitaries
engaged in their great office!
This, they declare, is

their day in the sun.

The parrots

Hear the parrots squawk.
Pay attention to their range
of well-worn phrases.

Hear them cough and screak.
Consider their raw parched throats.
One can grow weary

of the same refrain,
of daily obligations.
But it must be done.

It is parrot work.

The penguins

You're watching penguins
in a dream. The ocean roars
and crashes. They wait

and gaze mesmerised
by their own stillness and yours.
There is nowhere else.

Wait. Listen. No one
is waiting at the station
for you. No taxi.

The water's freezing.

The rats

In the high end store
they were quarrelling over
accessories and rats.

There was no shortage
of either, of all colours.
It was hard to choose

one appropriate
for the right circumstances.
So many gewgaws,

so few occasions.

Night Watch

River

Here comes the evening.
Let it settle in and wait
for something deeper

like the night ahead
with its convoluted dreams
from which you might wake

at any moment
swimming across the river
with its strange high banks

and scent of roses.

Dusk talk

Not long before night.
Half a moon in a clear sky
and evening cooling.

Very few in town
just a couple of runners
pounding the dead street.

We are where we are,
say the houses. Are you sure,
ask the gardens lost

in their own shadows.

Watchmaker

You turn the light off.
The clock spins like a lost child
in the new darkness.

Spin around again.
Where is the clock going now?
Who has wound it up?

The watchmaker rubs
his failing eyes. Time can wait
until he winds it

or the child is found.

Like clockwork

Night slips between days
as if they weren't there. Hours
flow away from you.

Here's the calendar
of wind and light. Time between
is an illusion

maintained by magic.
But flesh and sense keep moving,
yes, and organs too

function like clockwork.

The gates

Day empties itself
into night. All its contents
belong to darkness.

Night will rearrange
everything. None of this will
ever have happened.

Nothing has happened
after all, the battlements
are washed in clear light.

The gates are open.

In the streets of a small town

Parchment

In the bright sky, in
the brilliant sunlight, in
the town we are in,

we were out in streets
that were not exactly streets
but parchment. So time

turned into absence
and places that were places
and had proper names,

they too were parchment.

Ennui

A certain ennui
is bound to set in, they said
as they closed the door.

Ennui was charming.
The evening drew to a close
with perfect manners.

As night-time advanced
it grew colder and language
remained elegant

if a little bored.

The streets of a small town

How quiet it is
in the streets of a small town
when all are in bed.

Not quite everyone
of course. Some are walking home
or away from home

and there are the cars
tidying themselves away
into the silence

which is still waiting.

Stopping train

You have forgotten
the time of day, the dread hour
of the last meeting,

the day of the week,
the name of the long lost friend
who has now returned.

There is a hidden
country, a domain passed through
at night, on a train.

Should you have stopped there?

Love poem in plague time

Deep under this world
there should exist another,
complete in itself.

We should go there now,
while we have time and laughter
enough to fill it.

Let's drill down to it,
bringing with us our flowers,
plump, uproarious,

and brief as summer.

Adding up

Counting

First came the numbers
then the names, then the faces.
They had to count them

over and over
to make sure none were missing.
Then there were flowers

as there have to be,
so they counted the flowers
and counted again

in case they lost count.

Minutes

As if we could hear
their tiny feet pursuing
their imperative

of sweep and scurry
like insects ticking through blades
of deep silent grass.

Come closer darling
and listen with me as they
hone their manoeuvres.

Let's not count the hours.

Trainspotting

Death likes its records.
It works like a train spotter
watching from bridges.

The trains run under
the bridge. They are half empty.
The country stations

are silent with bare
platforms. The great terminus
is a vast hangar

waiting to fill up.

Figures

They read out figures
summoning figures. The cost
is not in figures.

The dust in the room
remains the dust in the room.
There is always dust.

Mouths move and eyes move.
Something is always moving
through dust and figures.

Mouths, eyes, breath, the cost.

Where there is sorrow

When there is sorrow
we will employ formal terms.
That is our office.

There will be anger
with its own formalities.
That is procedure.

There will be summer
and autumn. There will be wind
in the trees. There will

be a form for this.

In wartime

Speech bubble

When the minister
opens his mouth a darkness
emerges then fades

into the background.
Is it a failed speech bubble
or is it a thought?

How many people
are jostling in that darkness,
and do they then fade

into their own thoughts?

Wartime

There are profiteers
in the cupboard. There are thieves
in the neat hedgerows.

There are the rumours
and the alarms. It's the times
we live in they say.

Darling, these are days
of anxiety. Listen
to the high-pitched call

of small birds. Kiss me.

The enemy

Know your enemy,
they said. The whites of their eyes.
Start to learn their names.

There was fog that day
and we could not see their eyes.
Fields curled in grey mist.

Nothing had eyes. The names
we whispered were grass rustling
and a distant stream

we hadn't yet crossed.

Disasters of war

News of disaster
is normal. Normality
is the disaster.

This is disaster,
cries the headline, this being
wind, flood, fire and plague.

Here is where we live,
on the edge of the edge, light
in the heart of light,

among the shadows.

Ministry

At the Ministry
of Nothing there was little
of interest. Ghosts

flitted between rooms
and along wide corridors,
shivering with cold.

The past was gathered
in a debating chamber,
freezing as ever,

and the dead told lies.

In emergency

Emergency guide

Treat each question like
an exquisite piece of dirt.
Don't let it settle.

Wave your hands around
like a busy man trying
to make himself clear.

They know what you are
and what they expect from you.
You know what they are.

They are God. They wait.

Dry hands

Granted a briefing
with graphs, charts, speeches, questions,
approximations,

a sparrow blurts past.
a wasp fizzes against glass.
You don't touch your face.

The official sun
brawls into sight. A woman
wipes tears from her eyes

with hands like paper.

The future

The future will be
exactly as predicted.
There will be running

and darkness and rain
and a desperate longing
for a vanished past

as imagined by
old heads. Hands will touch,
lips meet, and someone

will sing aloud to the wind.

Fictions

Behind closing doors
the face draws back and the hand
moves into shadow.

The filming goes on.
The cameras are rolling
into deep fiction.

What does the script say?
Something is sure to happen.
That's what doors are for.

That's what fiction is.

Science fiction

The minister sweats.
There's nobody in the street
bar some friendly ghosts,

administering
angels, and sundry earthlings.
It's science fiction

in the suburbs. Now
the aliens have landed
there will be speeches,

fresh flowers, new myths

Uncertain terms

The angel of uncertainty

Somewhere in England
there are pantomime angels
taking possession

of shopping centres
and well kept civic gardens,
and here is their chief.

Hail and welcome back
Angel of Uncertainty.
Extend your wingspan

and sing as you must.

Addressing the nation

The scientists hold
out test tubes. Something's bubbling
on the frail tripod.

The experiments
are proceeding. The results
look to promise much.

A delegation
is waiting outside. Inside
the angels prepare

a neat show of wings.

Comic turn

When the very poor
laugh, something cracks in the world,
but it's not a joke,

or not exactly.
The secret of comedy
remains a secret.

It is in the rust
of the vocal cords, the smoke
of a dying world.

It's how you tell them.

Ozymandias

We rubbish ourselves
in celebration. We are
disjecta membra

of a lost body,
trunkless, headless, and legless,
in high fuck you mood.

Ozymandias
lived here once. There are his hands.
The sand runs through them

as empires once did.

Anger

In the street of nerves
the angry are gathering
for their festival.

There will be dancing,
of course there will be dancing,
yes, and accidents.

There will be bodies
in the street, not all of them
dancing, or twitching,

not all with anger.

After we died

Lush

Something had run out
of patience and excuses.
Time itself perhaps,

bleary, unsteady,
like the proverbial lush,
who can stumble on,

just sober enough
to recognise his own face
in a shop window

with the right lighting.

Bargain

Prevarications,
assurances, evasions…
the business of truth

drives a hard bargain
so they look to compromise.
In the cracked mirror

of the normal day
dust drifts between surfaces
and settles on skin

as if it were light.

Mouth

It's the moment words
become white noise in the mouth
that exhausts. Not lies

but the sound lies make.
Not the lack of clarity
or transparency

but the fleeting thought
of the crystal clear moment
before white noise comes,

before the mouth starts.

Blossom

It's as if dream had
blossomed into comedy.
There must be a script

for it, each moment
perfectly timed to explode
in fits of laughter

and exhaustion. Wind
prompts leaves and shadows to move
against a bright wall

like rapid writing.

After we died

On the day we died
they made it perfectly clear
that we had not died.

Nobody had died.
It was there in the records
that we had not died.

It was consoling.
We celebrated the fact,
or would have done so

had we been alive.

The consolations

Gift wrapped

The words have come back
to lodge in your ear. They're yours
but have been elsewhere.

Welcome home, you say.
Tell me about your travels.
What have you brought me?

We bring you distance,
they reply. Look, right there. See
those faint far miles?

Should we gift wrap them?

Sylph

Nymph. Salamander.
Sulphur. One might make a list,
a miscellany,

of words of delight,
of mere movements of the mouth
and be satisfied.

It's little enough
my love, this slightest stirring
of pleasure. Stay there.

Speak the words to me.

Diaphanous

The brilliant sunlight
hangs on the wall. The shadows
gently undulate

as in an old film
or a diaphanous gown.
Diaphanous. Time

hangs about the word.
How meekly words date and fade
as this too will fade

with its thin music.

Glory

Sometimes you hear it.
What? Nothing. *What do you mean?*
I mean just nothing,

the nothing between
that which signifies nothing
and where we must live,

somehow glorious
and nothing, full of itself.
What is it full of?

The glory. Nothing.

Unscripted

The streets are still bare.
The actors are not ready.
No one knows their lines.

No one has the plot.
What is to happen with them?
Where's the director?

Why not make it up?
Can't we improvise a script
out of all those lives?

Can't we just get dressed?

FIVE INTERLUDES

In praise of breathing

1

Breathing
is rococo.
It is effervescence
and invention, excessive, brief,
spangled.

2

Breathing
is secret. Breath
appears and vanishes.
It pirouettes on points. It glows
then dies.

3

Each breath
is distinct. Wait
for it. Encourage it
to indulge itself. Approve it.
Applaud.

4

To breathe
is to belong
to a privileged tribe.
May you be elected prince of
breathers.

5

I breathe.
You breathe. We breathe.
Does she breathe? Do they breathe?
The grammar of breath is simple
and harsh.

6

The dead
have stopped breathing.
Neither do they dance. Death
rhymes with breath. It is perfection.
It sings.

7

Beauty
is breathing in
a swimsuit. It is sleek
yet full figured. It has muscles
that pulse.

8

I sing
the beauty of
breath. I am the Whitman
of the lungs. I am Percy Bysshe
Shelley!

9

My breath
is the Sublime.
It is a Romantic
device. My breath is the west wind
in drag.

10

Let breath
prosper. Let it
swell the chest as it will.
Breathing is pure performance art.
Now breathe.

Hen Harrier

He with his black gloves
and she with her huge ringed fan
go riding the air.

Breathtaking the rise,
twist, swoop, sweep, drill of his flight,
the madness of it,

the capture, talons,
play and grasp of the feeding,
she like a fielder

in the slips, arching
backwards for the offering
off the finest edge

of the air. And cries,
the chiding and pecking strut
as they peel away.

I'm of the city,
with its lamppost trees and blind
windows over streets

of sun-struck car tops,
but no stranger to the breath
and fall of dancing.

These brief perfections
appear like dreams then vanish
into the dreamt room.

Too much of the world
lives in the dark and briefly
in that great blind rush

that burns like beauty
before its own clear mirror,
sharing the blear air.

Morning song

(for Martin Battye)

Behind the eyes, behind the glass, beyond the horizon
of the visible is plain and simple light, the fire and smear
of colour suffused with its own luminosity, its sense of self.

And there you stand at the very centre of it, blazed, lit,
blown, by the world in which you find yourself, alone
in the middle of Monet's field, of Seurat's riverbank,

of a lusciousness you may dive into or luxuriate in.
So the world moves, you say. So it shimmers at noon,
so it offers its prospects as through an open window.

Here you may meet the hedonistic angels of the hour
spent late in bed, vaguely aware of light through the curtains
as they hover around you with their silent brooding,

eventually rising, as you do, to the water in the bowl,
to the dazzle of the tablecloth, to the orange neatly peeled
and the spiritual comforts of cereal, toast and coffee.

This is a version of the world you may fully believe in.
These are the limits of what is unbounded yet disciplined,
even the darknesses of which offer a sort of glowing.

Time to open the post, to study the writing on the sheet
of paper before you, time to enter the full consciousness
of those crazy dimensions and then to clear the table.

Bear

1

A man made a bear in his likeness.
The bear's likeness was his bear.
It was a bear apart from other bears.
The man regarded the bear
And found in it his bearness

2

I have made this bear, thought the man.
And it is that bear that looks back at me,
Insisting on a bearness that is my insistence.

3

The bear sat at his side.
It was a comfort to him.
It was a comfort to the bear
To consider the man
As his companion.

4

The violence of the bear
Is my violence, said the man to the bear.
I have committed no violence said the bear
But you will, said the man. That is why I created you.

5

My fur is inward, said the bear, my claws also.
My claws are as real as you have made them, said the bear.
I bleed, said the man, But it is your blood that I bleed.
I am made to bleed, said the bear.

6

My kind is clawed and furred, said the man.
The earth is soaked in the blood we have shed.
I too am flesh and blood, said the bear.
I too am clawed and furred
But my claws and fur and teeth are my own
Beyond those that you invented.

7

We are one, said the man.
We are one, said the bear, who had no alternative.
One of us must suffer as a bear suffers.
One of us must suffer as a bear, one as a man.
I make the decisions round here, said the man.
I deal out the suffering.
No change then, said the bear in a stage whisper.

8

I am the Great Bear said the bear.
I am the Great Bear, said the man.
Have it your way, said the bear.

9

The bear was shrinking, the man was growing.
1 no longer need you, said the man.
Small bears are not my concern.

10

I dreamt of a man, said the bear.
I dream ever more of men.
Someone has to dream.

Dotage

Occasionally they hear dotage shuffling
up and down the hall, hesitating at the door
and asking in its feeble high-pitched voice
if it is time yet. *Is it time?* No, it is not,
they answer, straightening their backs.
Move away from the door, we need to use it.

And so it shuffles off, mumbling to itself,
disliking its own caricature gait
and ever less firm grip on irony
while they get on with life and slamming doors.

I see my father with his dotage grin
and watch as his eyes slowly turn to mine.
Get out, dad, I tell him, go now, while you can,
then realise he got out years ago.
I put my slippers on and comb my hair,
pleased to see how dark it is, like his.

There are doors leading to other doors,
they say, forgetting now to close them.

Dream of leaving

There they were, stuck in eternal sunlight,
With barely a quivering of leaves.
It was as if the clouds with all their benevolent rain
Had been stolen by a crowd of thieves.

Time did not move or rather it rushed by
In silence on dream-grease leaving behind
A cartoon panic played out in a cinema
At the back of the house in a broken mind.

Too many broken minds for lack of cloud
And shade. Too much stiffness in the solid air.
Nothing had moved inside the stifling house.
The best thing was to get right out of there.

Dream of delay

They were going to the city but the train
was late. There would be problems. What
to do now, to ring ahead and explain?
But would the bar be open then or shut?

Anxiety and anger led to drink.
They had the beer, there was a natural thirst
and night was coming on. Too late to think
of other trips, to see who'd come off worst.

It's always late, moaned Duncan. Paul agreed.
Then Mark piped up with a joke and Martin swore.
When it arrived the train was at half speed
and there'd be no point in going anymore.

The night weighed with them, heavy with its dirt.
There would be trouble. Someone would get hurt.

Dream of townscape

One talks of films and death.
Another listens to his heart.
Another is editing his own breath.
Another waits for his body to fall apart.

One talks of intimate matters
to innocent ears. One opens his mouth
to pour out a stream of incoherent letters
written in a friendless house.

One talks of starvation and disease
among birches. Another rides
horses in a circle of lush trees
where a terrible demon abides.

One parses a list of documents
while another dreams and yet another strolls
down a quiet street between events
clutching an account-book of lost souls.

One weeps, another does not.
Another's mind goes blank.
One must conduct an exercise
where the living march in rank

There are ghosts in town tonight.
Let the mayor compose a speech.
Let him be effusive so his bright
words greet those he still can reach.

One must run an orderly town.
One must pay bills while another must beg.
Another must put on a dressing gown
before boiling an egg.

This is a film. This is a body. This
the script and commentary.
This is the moment of paralysis.
This is nothing. This is memory.

Dream of screaming

There were people running screaming down
the street the way they always scream
when running. He heard them in his head
and screamed with them, his scream
melting into theirs, into the silence under
the screaming, and the silence after.

But the screaming continued long after
the running. It was the sky they were under
and the perfection under the scream.
Already people were running through his head
screaming, *Scream, damn you! Scream!*
into the silence they were running down.

Dream of dystopia

I woke up in dystopia, it was bad,
just like the warnings said, but so much worse,
around me sat the nightmares I had had,
and all the future, too late to reverse.

Dystopian fields as far as the eye could see,
destruction, rust, dead trees, polluted streams.
I'd seen them all on screen repeatedly,
surfing along the underside of dreams.

I have imagined that I've woken up,
I told myself, and maybe I was right.
If films can start they can as surely stop.
Don't cower there, don't swathe yourself in night.

Man up, I said. I pulled myself together.
and set off to explore the filthy weather.

Dream of television

I woke up dead and turned on the TV
and there I was. The rumours were all true.
That face was mine – how could it not be me? –
I gazed at it and said, *Yes, that is you.*

But I was like another, with a name
I could not speak, another who was dead.
I was the child I had been, still the same:
my eyes, my mouth, my ears, my nose, my head.

You see nuncle, it said, *we are the same
but who that is I really cannot say.
I'm just the dead and I don't have a name.
Let's meet again*, it said and turned away.

Dream of Moldova

I woke in a bedroom in Moldova,
The mirror was broken, the door locked,
The street was empty and the window frosted,
No soap in the bathroom and the sink was blocked.

Fake news, said the light in my brain.
Trust me, it's fake, it repeated.
Moldova is a story and location
That can be redacted or deleted.

But this is my bedroom, I protested.
This is Moldova as it was meant to be.
The mirror here is genuinely broken,
The place exists in its own reality.

You call things names, said the voice, but names
Are objects we drop and they sometimes break.
This is the news: this the alternative.
The real may be real but this is fake.

We're in a bad place, I thought and lay down
On the bed. *We arrive any old how*.
Then fell asleep and dreamt of mirrors
And endless streets in downtown Chisinau.

Dream of the Danube

We could ride over the Danube
or sit on the step watching melon-rind drift down the tide
in a summer that is intolerable
while the city is half-asleep or sheltering
near the railway track a long way from the city
which is a long way to whatever music is sung in its tunnels
by the dead who must live there
but rarely appear on the platform
we enter through the doors of the Metro
where the nearest waterfall is an escalator descending
the other rising in the throat
into the light of midday
where a hot-air balloon is a heart
to a cavity to exhaustion to coffee
to the rococo pastry of the lungs.

BESTIARY

Orpheus

Oh, to charm the birds off the trees!
To sing so everything follows.
Son of Calliope, hand us the keys
To the house of mysteries.

I would love to have sung to demons, he said, or she
said, in the dim light of the pub. One loses voices in
the dark. One just sings. Or one turns the lights right
off and tells stories to a room that has suddenly grown
dense. That is the house of mysteries. That is where
the dancers perform and tear you limb from limb. It is
the animal kingdom without dictionary or *catalogue
raisonné*. It is where you live.

Ass

Speak to the load you bear
And to our patience, ever lacking.
Play Balaam to our dictionary
And send us packing.

In the donkey dictionary there are only brays, long or short, loud or quiet. Donkey poetics are as much duration as stress. The donkey Alexandrine and the donkey pentameter are only feet after all. The verb 'to bray' is as packed with ambiguities as the donkey itself. Someone has to bear the blame for this, someone has to carry the can. Open your mouth. Let the clear voice of reason emerge.

Lion

Dance, rampant lion. Fling your mane
And roar, so nature flinches.
Stride about the world again
And make it yours by inches.

It was our first lion and we were determined not to
lose it. We tracked it along the savannah in an old jeep
covered with crude portraits of film stars. Clark Gable's
image decorated the grille. Dorothy Lamour was on the
tailgate. Charles Laughton and Bud Abbott were on the
doors, and Mary Pickford on the hood. If Hollywood
was on our side nothing could happen to us. Then the
lion came striding and we reversed into a handy nearby
garage. We had forgotten the Andrews Sisters.

Stag Beetle

Horned demon, stag beetle,
Half insect, half Swiss-army-knife,
Your armour seems impregnable.
Have you come to take my life?

I have lived among insects all my life, he said, handing
me a stag beetle. It was a magnificent specimen, a martial
object equipped for both defensive and offensive oper-
ations. When propped up at 45 degrees it suggested a
renaissance nightmare, the perfect rejection of humanism,
but now, in my palm it simply sat like a philosophical
problem. But there would be a solution, he said. There
would be lots of solutions.

Fire Lion

Ever emerging out of the dark
Of the mental forest, your head
Of flames brings light and intolerable
Heat, like setting fire to my bed.

The Fire Lion is to be found among your books, an
incendiary waiting for the final conflagration. I can see
one behind your brow right now stalking you like a
giant apprehension. It won't stay there. It will emerge
from your mouth, stately and terrifying. The books
will burn of course but other books will rise from the
ashes. The lion too will rise, the book of perfections in
its mouth, its mind ablaze with the mottoes it finds
there.

Ram skull

The skull curled about itself, worn
As ornament, as bass clef, as strut
And thrust. How have you become
An image? How come you snap shut?

The ram is an orchestra by itself, a shofar, a bukkehorn.
It resounds through the hall of mirrors that is God's
house. There several reflected rams perform an arcane
dance choreographed by Busby Berkeley. The politics
may be dubious but their clear music is unmistakeable.
Bring on the ram's horn. Wear it on your own head.
Command the available space.

Toad

Let me versify you into life,
In your oilskin coat, with your outspread toes.
I want to feel you leap right through my chest
Like phlegm in my mouth and nose.

Between wall and fence, in a puddle of its own, the toad squatted. It must have been about important business because it barely noticed me and did not look up at my approach. You will have to sit down and wait your turn, I can't do everything at once, it eventually remarked. So saying it leapt into my open mouth and began to dictate affairs. It was only when I sneezed that it politely made its exit and settled back into a damp pocket of the universe.

Chauve Souris

More trace than body, more dusk than night,
Nothing like bird or mouse in your address,
I imagine a huge hand crushing you
Into a speck, infinitely more of less.

The bat had flown in through the window and was now tangled in the open curtains. The city lay below us with the sleeping river, the domes and spires of the prevalent religion next to the great juggernauts of commerce, all its nightlife crawling down the street or scurrying along like defenceless mice. It was then the bat cried out and the curtains began to flap. The bat was still struggling. It was like an apple core with leathern wings. Leathern was a word we had found in the guidebook, appropriate for just such occasions.

Owl as anagram

Crone of the Goddess, Wol, anagram
Of Low, good luck to you and us.
Bring us the mice we require, Minerva.
Feed the carnivorous!

It sat in the middle of the road, temporarily dazzled by
the oncoming headlights that it must have taken for the
eyes of an enormous owl. The wood was full of owls,
all watching, appraising the event with admirable self-
control. The forest floor was littered with dead creatures,
prey of some sort. Nobody was waxing sentimental about
the owl, about any owl, least of all the one in the middle
of the road.

Ant

May we address any one of you by name,
Jack, Susan, David, Rose, and Beth?
Something creeps up the spine, like shame,
Nameless presences: work, scurrying, death.

We thought they were letters but they were ants. The
book they were writing was the Ant Directory. Someone
told us they were the dead of two world wars but they
kept jostling about the page writing ever more names.
This is their memorial, it said on the title page. They
are dead but they will answer if you call, unless they
are ex-directory, in which case you will have to call
someone else. I consider my dead: Jack, Susan, David,
Rose, Beth, Alfred, Danny, Amy, Xavier, Baby, Ronald.

Ram

The beauty of horror, the horror of beauty.
Somewhere at the back of the Gothic ark
Lies the imagination, a frcight of bones
And lightning in the terminal dark.

Her head was upside down. She was clearly a Goth.
Goth was the fashion of the time and generally
involved some level of evisceration. She told me her
name was Nosferatu and spat a small bullet of blood at
my shoes. A woman ran shrieking down the hall while
a ghost was vainly trying to push its way through the
wall in pursuit of her. Are you Charles Bukowski,
asked a young girl clamouring for an autograph. Good
heavens no, I said. I am not fit to touch the hem of his
garment.

Emerging life form

Like the alien bursting from John Hurt's stomach
So nature haunts the artificial moon.
The place is crawling with emergence,
A caterpillar in its slick cocoon.

I was born on a Friday and have ever since regretted it.
Bound in slime I sat on the floor, helpless with desire.
The days were passing but there was no change in my
circumstances. I couldn't move. I couldn't escape. There
was no one around to help me. There was only the moon
in the window like a head without a face. This can't be
everything, I thought. It is not what I came for.

Chained beast

Slouching towards Bethlehem to be born,
He hesitates before heaving a great sigh.
It need not always be so troublesome
To reach your destination and to die.

I will tell you when it's time for a new god, he said.
For now you will have to make do with that snarling
mass of impotence in the cage there. The old god
looked at me, its eyes surprisingly benign. It was a
little unkempt. No one had brushed its mane or picked
the lice off its ears. Forgive my appearance, it said. I
was not always as you see me now. I had a suit, a hat,
a decent pair of shoes. I smelled of death. Behind my
eyes, in the far distance, you could make out a battle-
field full of crows and broken standards.

Tortoise

Carapace, plastron, crepuscular...
Your vocabulary crawls from under the tongue
The way you do between rocks.
I am your lyre, the song that goes unsung.

In one of Ovid's forgotten metamorphoses Orpheus is
turned into a tortoise. He has retreated into his shell
and it takes the Maenads to entice him out. It doesn't
end well. It never does. But the music remains, echoing
in his shell as under a helmet. That is what tragedy is
for.